Brown Bag Poetry

TERRY LYLE

Order this book online at www.trafford.com/08-0982
or email orders@trafford.com

Most Trafford titles are also available at major online book retailers.

Edited by Tracy Duke Arnold.
Cover Design by Justin Pooler.
Photography by Terryatte E. Lyle.

Note for Librarians: A cataloguing record for this book is available from Library and Archives Canada at www.collectionscanada.ca/amicus/index-e.html

ISBN: 978-1-4251-8455-1

www.trafford.com

North America & international
toll-free: 1 888 232 4444 (USA & Canada)
phone: 250 383 6864 ♦ fax: 250 383 6804 ♦ email: info@trafford.com

The United Kingdom & Europe
phone: +44 (0)1865 487 395 ♦ local rate: 0845 230 9601
facsimile: +44 (0)1865 481 507 ♦ email: info.uk@trafford.com

10 9 8 7 6 5 4 3 2

About the authoress…

Terry E. Lyle is a happy go lucky female whose goal is to be wealthy and wise. Terry has the natural ability to bring you tears and laughter while reaching down to those hidden emotions with a slap of reality. Brown Bag Poetry was inspired by her many travels throughout the United States and abroad. She has an uncanny ability to write about life's experiences as seen through various employments in her lifetime in fields such as, Law Enforcement, Medical, Education, and Transportation. Terry is a Christian who is passionate about church, children, and moral values. She resides in Phenix City, AL, but hails from Baltimore, MD. One of her favorite quotes is, "Either get busy living, or get busy dying, choose life; because God has a purpose and plan for your life. He loves you". Life is too short to waste a minute, so press forward, relax, and enjoy yourself. [Smooches]

Dedication

With much love and respect,
I dedicate all my work, first to the glory of God,
my loving, patient,
and always devoted mom, Mrs. Lola M. Robertson
Matthews, and my very special friend;
A source of inspiration, and sunshine,
who has helped me from beginning to end,
throughout the whole process and with a listening ear,
Mrs. Tracy Duke Arnold, known to me as
"Ms. Lady Bug." Thank You!

Acknowledgements

I would like to thank Steve Harvey for his Godly, inspirational words that got me off of my lazy butt in April of 2008.

Also

To my crazy, unpredictable, loving family; My mother Lola M. Matthews, brothers Stanley & Phillip Robertson, my sisters Sylvia Robertson and Deidra Jacqueline Robertson (deceased), Mrs. Nichole Sylvia Lyle-Crapper my only and dearly loved daughter, my beautiful precious grandchildren; Jaguar, Jermeanez, Javon, Jakotae, and Jabari, I give you the best part of me. My two nephews, Christian & Shawn Robertson (deceased).

I must not forget the protection and guidance from my grandparents Elisha and Irene Robertson (deceased), Aunts Carol L. Robertson and Sarah Murphy, and my dear Uncles Elisha and Bennie Robertson. In loving memory of relatives past, Aunts Flossie Mae Cooper, Roxie A. Mitchell House, and Margaret V. Motes, and Uncle Floyd Robertson.

I also mustn't forget

my friends growing up in the old neighborhood on the 2100 block of Lexington street in Baltimore, Maryland, especially Warren McNeil. Also my home girls, once I blossomed, Mabel "Elaine" Douglas, Cheryl E. Dixon and Angela Morris. And I will not forget, my sister girl Pearlie "PEACHES" Grant. (I Love You).

Welcome

to

Brown Bag Poetry

Enjoy your reading!

Tables of contents

(Adult explicit poems will be preceded by an asterisk *)

In the Beginning

Back in the beginning, when God created man
Because of his awesome wisdom, he had a great plan.
He created the heavens, the earth, the moon, and the stars
He created all things, below and above.
God even created time, just for you and me
So we could enjoy, this wonderful.... Opportunity
Unfortunately, like everything else
Man made a big mistake

Did what he wanted and just wouldn't wait.
Now because of this, death has claimed her stake
And many lives will go to her because of Eve's mistake.
The body count is rising at every turn and wake.
The things we seemed to used to love now it seems we love to
Hate

We used to live hundreds of years and now it's down to a few.
We've inherited sickness, pain, death, mental illness, and crazy
folks like you, also acquired the diseases like Polio and the flu.
Have heart conditions, strokes, diabetes, including paranoia too....
Now our mindsets have been corrupted, and our marriages,
they don't last.

Our problems started out long ago because Eve acted out too fast.
Doing what she knew was wrong, she was warned what not to do
She even encouraged that stupid Adam, to eat the apple too.
Now both were kicked out of the garden and sent out on their own...

But thank God for salvation..... Because Jesus called us home.

Barack Obama

Barack Obama is a black man, born into meager means. He is now running for the office of the United States Presidency. His opponent was a very strong white woman named Hillary Clinton; plus she wasn't kidding. She ran this race hard. Girlfriend was in it to win it. Hillary ran a really good race and she kept her issues all up in his face. Now Barack is a strong man as well. The validity of his issues, he also could sell. Barack makes a lot of sense and he's here to make a change. His promises, this country really hopes he can arrange. President Bush really screwed the United States up; now people are running scared, towards lottery for luck. Everything is sky high and it's really a mess. President Bush called this depression an economic test. Barack Obama is now on the scene, he ran a great race, while keeping it clean. History was made in two thousand and eight. Now I hope we don't have much longer to wait; to change the theorem that has existed too long, where a black man can't be president; that theory is gone.

No Answer

I don't know why you insist on calling, you must like to waste your time, because if you are at a pay phone, I'm sorry you lost some dimes. People like us should never be allowed to use the phone because we hardly ever use the thing because we never stay at home. But, you can leave a message if you like, ha ha ha ha…, and if I don't return your call, then simply try to write.

Race Card

Don't play the race card because it isn't a game. It's not for entertainment, just humility and shame. Don't talk about minorities, whites, blacks, or the Jews, because when you talk about others, they will talk about you. This injustice has been going around way too long. It's time we change and let bygones be gone. People have been beaten, murdered, raped and abused, cheated out of their possessions, so they never win, but lose; just hated because of the color of their skin, never trying to see the person that lives within. When you hold resentment because of something in your past, doing stuff like this is the reasons that racism lasts. Let's see each other for who we are.... another human being who deserves your love. Let's make some changes and let's make them today, it's been so much time wasted, so let's not delay. Don't play the race card and don't play it today.

Just Me

In the stillness of the night, I find myself unable to sleep, sprawled across my bed while I watch my chest rise and fall, breathing slow and effortlessly. Softly I caress the smoothness of my skin, ever so gently. Then I slowly close my eyes as my eyelids flutter like a butterfly in flight. I reach upwards and cup my breast between my hands while paying close attention to the occasional pinching of my nipples, shyly peeping out as to be noticed. My fingertips begin the journey upwards slowly, gently, to trace the outlines of my mouth, as my lips begin to spread at the tingle of my touch. I find myself drifting off to the place where I laid next to your nakedness with my mouth licking your skin velvet unto my tongue, where nothing matters, and time stands still. I pull and squeeze in a sucking motion upon your flesh as I grip it between my hands. It's hard to catch my breath, and while arching my back I feel like I'm falling into nothingness. I sigh with moans of lust escaping my lips and moisture oozes over and consumes my body. Beads of sweat glisten upon my brow. No longer can I contain the pulsating rhythms within the walls of my vagina, needing to feel your hands upon my body, while lying close in our nakedness. Heat rises from my neck in the dead silence of the night. My nipples press against the moisture of your skin, stuck as if we're molded into one. I bite my lip while I moan with pleasure beyond my wildest dreams, climbing so high, I can't breathe, as I feel a rush of hot pulsating liquids oozing slowly from me, and I've lost all track of time, not sure of where I'm at, but not wanting to leave there, unable to breathe, longing to linger while the thickness is in the air of our hot passionate sex. I slowly inhale in an effort to cool down from the fire burning inside of me, longing for an ice cube to drip its coolness upon me, as the water runs down between my breasts to the cradle of my navel. You lick my inner thigh, as I struggle to find the strength to continue; stroking the hair upon your neck and your tongue darts out to tease the lips of my vagina with your playful motion. I heave my body upward towards your sensuous, hot, moist tongue, waiting for you to penetrate me deeply, when I realize, I'm alone, and it's just me.

Life

Balled up so tight in my fetal position; barely moving, listening to the sounds of the night air. Tick tock tick tock, a slow hum, my eyes flutter but shapes are just blurred images. I won't move; I feel safe in this comfort zone. I stretch to get comfortable and I hear a low murmur of voices.

My ears tingle, and my heart races. I wonder, "Is there an intruder in the next room." I feel panic and frozen in my fears. I have to escape because the voices are getting louder, and I see a flickering of light just over my shoulders.

Instinctively I crouch down and duck my head, looking for a safe place to hide.

Oh my God, a burst of light enters my hiding place. My heart races, I'm flushed and nervous. I can't speak, nothing comes out. Help I think, yell help, hurry. But all I do is cry, suddenly I'm attacked, I'm grabbed, pulled on, and hit, while everyone watches, the noise around me intensifies, and a blur of faces surround me. I don't know what to do.

Oh no. A blanket is thrown over me, what is this I think, "What is going to happen to me." In the midst of the people, a man reaches out and picks me up, and carries me away. I fear the worst. My life is never going to be the same I thought. Then reality hit me when I hear, "Mrs. Lyle, meet your beautiful baby girl."

Roses

Today I received a phone call. I was asked by the person on the line.... was it me that they called by name, to whom they were speaking to.... Now in my mind, I'm thinking, "yeah right, another person trying to get me to contribute to their cause, or someone trying to offer me some type of credit card deal." I replied, "Who wants to know?" After a few seconds, I got the response, "it's a florist shop, trying to make a delivery." Immediately I got excited. I wondered, "Did I win the publisher's clearing house sweepstakes and would the prize patrol arrive at my door with balloons, roses, and a big fat check". I'm so excited, I run to the door, checking and looking up and down the street, waiting for my delivery. Primping and fixing my clothes for the photographers on the camera crew, my excitement was so infectious. I couldn't stop smiling and waving at all of the vehicles traveling up and down the road while perfecting my princess wave. Nervously, I get up...sit down.... Pace backwards and forwards. Finally, a florist's van pulls up. There are neither balloons nor fanfare, as they approach my steps with the most beautiful floral arrangement. I wonder in awe, "who could have possibly sent this and what's the occasion." Hesitantly, I pull out the card to read, "Have a nice day; hold your head up." I realize they were from my best friend. I didn't need to win any sweepstakes because I'm already a winner. I've been blessed with more than money can buy... I have a loving friendship; how priceless? I realized that when I saw the rose.

Peeping and Creeping

There you go, back and forth, just a looking and acting lost.
I don't know what kind of game you're playing,
but my patience's been tossed.

Here you are peeping and creeping, driving up and down,
and you call yourself sneaking.

What are you looking for and what's the deal?
You know people who lie, they also steal.

My momma told me a long time ago,
"Whatever you reap, you will sow. So why you're sitting there chasing
behind me, keep looking long enough, something you'll see.

Some people have too much time on their hands, doing dumb stuff or
acting grand. When you're peeping and creeping and looking for trouble,
that's when your issues, they start to double.

So don't get mad when I curse you out, because this silly stuff,
I'm not about.

So when you're peeping and creeping, while looking for trouble,
acting paranoid, yet not too subtle,

Remember this and remember it well, you can kiss my ass…
and go to hell…

Believe

Are you on drugs? And if it is so, I'm sure you know
Your mind is the first thing to go.
Nothing makes sense in the things you say,
Yet you continue to get high anyway.
Your money is spent trying to get a fix,
while paying for withdrawals that are making you sick.
Caught up stealing and breaking the law,
Your life is at risk.... most of all.
Hoping you can change the lifestyle you see,
in and out of rehab, unfortunately.
This battle can be won, that you will see,
But, first my friend, you must trust and believe.

Boredom

Bored again! How do I explain this? We all go through it; for me, it's extremely hard. My personality is hyper, upbeat, borderline; goofy, and even considered intense. I love life and being part of it. The sun on my face is like a vacation in paradise; so many things to do and people to see. The only thing that will slow me down with my routine is running out of gas. Prices so high, the shock sends you into depression. Boredom gives you the opportunity to think and reflect and depression does the same; you're just sadder. I've given this some thought and it seems when you're bored, you look for things to do, but when you're depressed, you give up and don't want to do anything. I still find myself alone with nothing to do and not really happy with that prospect. So I was just thinking, "am I bored or depressed?"

I Don't Care

Have you ever met the woman that makes your heart skip, have you smiling just because they are near; yet you hold back because she belongs to another. You yearn to touch her supple breast and draw her body close to you, as you daydream a rush of sweet smelling air passes by, like unto a whisper upon your cheek.

You look up and see your dream girl leaving. As you inhale and decide to go and engage in small talk before the door opens to her escape. Your feet refuse to move, planted as in cement, try as you might, they won't bulge.

You open your mouth to speak, as you see the door begins to open, then from behind someone grabs your shoulder, and calls out your name, "stop", they said, "don't move, are you trying to kill yourself, stepping out into traffic like that?"

As you turn around, you realize this is the anniversary of the death of your wife, your dream girl, and you respond, "I don't care."

My Heart

When we talk, often there are a lot of emotions just below the surface. Can you hear the crack in my voice as I masquerade my tears and chalk it up as allergies. Do you hear the words with your ears or can you hear my heart? My heart is shy and often takes a back seat to what my brain instructs my lips to say. Take heed and listen closely when my heart speaks, it's soft and humble, but the message is very powerful. My heart shies away from confrontation and rarely wants to be on the front line. My heart is small in size; very fragile, and bruises easily, if not handled with care. Blinded by the light, my heart reaches out, seeking a resting place. Just like Braille, sensitively tracing the outline of yours, hoping that together, two hearts will be synchronized; beating to the same tune. "You for me and me for you."

Death

This statement is true and not a lie. We are all born, just to die.
Death is something that will never wait. When it comes for you, it won't be late. When we are sick, we prepare for the worst, but if death knocks, the pain still hurts. Things are a little easier if you have insurance, but if you don't it becomes an annoyance. Having to plan a funeral through tear stained eyes; you're emotionally drained and just want to cry. Things you wish you could have said, they remained locked still inside your head. Regrets, I'm sure there's a few, but the suffering really doesn't suit you. As you travel down memory lane, you wish for those happy times again. You've been told that it gets better in time, receiving words of encouragement from people that's kind. With this being said, I'll say this, my friend, when death knocks at your door, don't let him come in.

Mousetrap

I know this guy, he is truly a rat
When he leaves my home, he takes forever to get back.
Boyfriend be smelling like a cologne that's not mine
When "I" want to talk, he doesn't have the time.
When the phone rings, he looks guilty as hell.
It must be some chick, but how can I tell?
Sweating bullets and can't even talk,
He takes the phone while he whispers and walks.
Somebody must have told him wrong,
Home girl is fed up, and he's about to be gone.
I've been through this shit too many times before,
I can smell a rat, when he walks through the door.
So listen up fool, if you want to act like a rat,
Just trust and believe, I will be your mouse trap.
Snap............

Kindergarten Years

As a kid I didn't realize that I would have to go
to a place with many faces that I didn't even know.
They gave me snacks on a tray. I even had some fun,
because they would let me play… and I would run and run and run.
I got kind of used to the faces, that I would often see
I met Tommy, Joyce, and also Melanie
My mother would come and get me a little later in the day
She took me home, to take a nap, no longer could I play.
But that was ok when I was young and had nothing really to do.
Because I'm older now, I realize that was school.
The beginning of my learning, in things I needed to know,
was in the Kindergarten, where my mind began to grow.

"Thank you Mommy, Thank you Daddy."

I'm

I'm watching TV, all by myself, and I'm watching TV,
while I am undressed.
I'm wearing my panties, but I'm not wearing my bra,
because you see I won't venture far.
I'm sprawled across the bed, trying to get some rest,
and would you believe it, yeah, my hair is a mess.
I have a bottle of water, lying right next to my butt,
It isn't cold any longer, but oh, so what?
I'm scratching my arms, because they itch, I feel real moody,
but I won't bitch.
I pigged out on candy, to satisfy my sweet tooth,
even though I knew the sucker was loose.
Now my mouth is in pain, and I'm mad as hell,
because I was stupid, as you can tell.
So the moral of this story, I guess it is this... You know sometimes...
life sucks and it really ain't shit.

Behind Bars

You're locked up, yet you make demands.
What makes you think, you control my plans?
Calling collect and getting on my nerves,
with the same old crap I've already heard.
Complaining because you haven't received any mail;
forgetting it's your fault that your ass is in jail.
When you break the law, don't get mad,
when you think about your old life, it wasn't so bad.
Now you're serving five to ten,
behind bars where you can't pretend
that this problem wasn't really your fault;
after all, you're the one who robbed the vault
on that really crazy day,
when the police...., took your ass away.

Church Steps

I'm standing on the church steps, a sinner, afraid to go in. Looking for salvation, I heard I'd find with him. Longing for relationship... with Jesus Christ you see, because I've been told by many, he died for you and me.

As I approached the opened door, the usher motioned me in. I thought about how long in church, I had never been. So this was a little frightening, because I knew not what to expect, but I knew to bring some money, cause that they will collect.

I found a seat on a row, all the way in the back, afraid to be noticed, so that is where I sat. The music seemed so wonderful and the sermon I thought was great, and when they opened the doors to the church, I knew I couldn't wait.

I rushed down to the altar, and laid my burdens down and that is where I felt the glory, of the man who wore the crown.

As tears streamed down my face, I gave Jesus all the praise, and gave my life over to him, that wonderful, frightful day.

And now I usher at the door, as the people are filing in, can't wait to tell the story about the day I met the King.

Being Realistic

I'm an undiscovered treasure waiting to be found.
I'm right in reach, but you won't turn around.

I have so many qualities that you would adore,
but you like misery and pacing the floor.

I'm like a jewelry box; waiting to be opened, you miss out on me,
while thinking you're coping.

My inner light, it shines so bright, I'm not Misses Wrong, I'm Misses Right.

You think my affections that I have for you will allow you
to treat me like a comfortable shoe.
How wrong you are and let's get it right, baby I'll be long gone,
and way out of sight.

I don't have stupid written on my head.
So let's put this stupid thought to bed.
I must admit I think you are great,
but no longer on you am I willing to wait.

I'm going to pack my love up cause I'm ready to go,
have to do what I must, and do what I know.
I'm going to find my dream mate, who's waiting for me,
because of my inner beauty they will see.

So as I said, and I'll say it again, you'll never know what might have been.

And I'm just …. "Being realistic"!

Anticipation

What a great way my day is starting off. The weather is beautiful and I'm feeling good about myself. I have a few dollars in my purse…while the best part of this is …when the night comes…talk about anticipation. Let me explain my excitement. I'm going to have a date this evening. The thought makes my panties moist, just thinking about it. Now this brother is taller than me, well dressed, attractive, smooth conversation, and smells so good. He's like gravy that I want to sop up with a biscuit; just all around
H-O-T…Hot!!! Just like smoke in a fire, totally overwhelming. Now I'm preparing for tonight. I've pulled out my sexy lace underwear, no bloomers for me tonight, No, No!...I'll take a hot, sweet smelling pineapple bubble bath, douche my inside, pamper my feet, and shave all the nuisance hair off my body. I intend to be smooth and soft as a baby's behind, ready to be spanked like a big girl, Oh yes! I am waiting and ready for his hot lips and tongue to search out the area between my thighs to where my pussy is moist and ready for him to devour me, very slow and rhythmically. His hands will engulf my breasts, as he pinches my nipples, while the intensity of the moment will have me pulsating. I'll wish that he would replace his tongue with his penis, that's so hard and rigid, as he mounts me like a jockey breaking in a new stallion. As his semen oozes out of the head of his dick, slimy and wet into my vagina, my hands slide up and down the length of his muscular back, as his rock hard penis thrust into me deeply back and forth with his balls

slapping the outside of my pussy like in a tennis match, being served. As I cling to his back, I'm enjoying this sensuous explosive wild ride of ecstasy, my breathing is labored; I am sweaty, and convulsing in pleasure as I visualize in anticipation.

I Look

I look at you and my heart flutters. I feel like a teenager, unsure of what I should say, or how it would sound. I want to glance your way, but I don't want to stare. I feel myself drawn to you.

Your lips I wonder are they as soft as they look. Your smile draws me near you. I breathe heavy with anticipation of what's going to happen next. I try to compose myself, and keep the shy side of me hidden, but my nerves are jumping up and down with excitement.

I get in line, to wait my turn, hoping when I get to the counter it's you who waits on me. I try to pretend I'm busy doing nothing, so I avoid eye-contact All the while something just draws me to you.

A smile creeps across my lips; I've made it to the front of the line, and your smile, and arms gesture for me to come closer. Oh how I wish I could embrace you, but I just make small talk.

I think I'm being clever, with my jokes and conversations, when all of a sudden you cracked on me. "You act like you're attracted to me, what, did the Devil make you do it? You said with a chuckle.

I wonder; does she really know how I feel or is it a lucky guess, or small talk back at me? I become nervous. And I think "damn girl, I was thinking the same thing."

I thought, "I have to shake my head on this one, the jury is still out, just my damn luck, you walked into my destiny."

But that's how the stars lined up. Fate is what it is. It takes you to your crossroads.

Begging

I'm driving home from a long day in church. My phone rings, it's another plead to borrow money again. It seems like a mess I have gotten myself into; what a nightmare. Before I had given money to my neighbors that was supposed to be a loan; how wrong I was. I have never been reimbursed. I let it go because it was small amounts, but now it's a nuisance. My neighbors have other adults living there, yet they hunt me down to beg for money. Cigarettes and alcohol, I don't do, it's not my place to support the vices of someone else. It seems to me that if you can't afford to smoke, then you need to stop. I truly have compassion for my neighbors and people I encounter during the course of my day and try to help those that are in need. Please give me a break, while on my money I wait.

Mothers and Daughters

Precious memories! Oh they seem so long ago.
I still remember you as a baby that I kissed, hugged, and hold.

Now my baby doesn't understand me, and we argue, fuss, and fight,
and sometimes there's screaming, all through the night.

Don't seem to know just how to make this bad situation right,
because nothing can be accomplished when we argue, fuss, and fight.

My daughter's growing up so fast, and won't take the time to look.
Beware of the danger signs out there; I've learned from the steps
that I took.

Trying to fill shoes baby that your feet are too small to fill;
Life will offer you pitfalls, as well as some thrills.
I try to protect you and give you all the wisdom that I can;
protect your internal power and don't give it to any man.

One day I hope, after shedding a few tears that you'll grow to understand;
all I wanted to give you was my love, for that was my only plan.

You will always be my baby, and I'll always be right here.
Waiting to guide you, and have a listening ear.

Some days you make me angry and I wish I could turn back the hands of
the clock. On those different days, when we didn't scream, argue,
fuss and fight.

When time has passed and you're fully grown, I hope you remember these
little things you've learned and share them with your own.

You

With anticipation I came by to see you; as you opened the door,
I looked into your eyes. They sparkled as you came closer to greet me.

I followed you around like a puppy dog, just wanting to be where you are.
You touched my hand, and I smiled, just like you've touched my heart.

We laughed, talked, and enjoyed the company of each other.
It was all about you.

With expectation as I sat across the room from you, I thought how
I wanted to feel you; I got my courage up and came towards you.

As I embraced your face, I kissed your soft lips while I sucked softly on
your tongue, not wanting the kiss to end, but last forever.

Time has come for my departure, and the memories they will last forever,
as I think about how wonderful my day was, because it was all about you.

Christians

Everyone wants to be a Christian and some act like they are, but the real deal, we all fall short. We're just like everyone else and have the same problems; kids on drugs, abusive relationships, infidelity, chatter-box mentality, drunkenness, and homosexuality.

Try as we might to live in a spiritual realm, we see this earthly existence constantly pulling at us, always in the fire while the devil excites us with hidden pleasures such as, lottery addictions, profanity and dishonesty. We continue to go to the house of the Lord to worship and seek a healing, searching for that peace that passes all understanding that we've heard about since the beginning of time. With broken spirits and a contrite heart we continue daily seeking the Word. Subtle changes emerge in your makeup. You cry less, your strength begins to return. You become more helpful, you retain bible verses, you give your life over to Christ and get baptized and you realize you are a Christian but we all fall short and fall down... So, fellow saint, get up and just STAND!!!

Keepsakes

Keepsakes are precious items of memories past.
Things you cherish and hope they last.
Keepsakes you hold very dear.
It's noticed that you love them, it's apparently clear.
Keepsakes you dust off and handle with care.
So your treasure will last from year to year.
Keepsakes can be pictures, jewelry, furniture, or whatnots.
They are things that are small or a lot.
Keepsakes of the heart are also true.
When I think of keepsakes, I think of you.

Dinner Party

Do you think because I care that it's ok to have me at your beck and call? When you smile and glance my way, my heart grows tender as I long to embrace you. My time is consumed with your every wish as if I was a genie in a lamp and you rub the emotions of my soul.

While I ponder this thought, I reach inward and dig deep into my pockets to reveal my dollars; crumpled and balled up as I race to the grocery store as the light of the day begins to darken.

Aisle by aisle I look for that bargain. I have a special dinner to prepare. I'm so embarrassed, I only have twelve dollars, but this must work; I have until 8:00 pm to prepare dinner.

In a whirlwind my head is spinning making decisions on how I can feed four people with twelve dollars. I stare at the empty cart while I wheel myself from aisle to aisle.

Ok six dollars on pot roast, two dollars on can vegetables, great, I think, and I spend one fifty on a bag of rice. Wow just $9.50, I'm doing well, so I splurge on an onion for sixty cents.

I'm feeling hopeful, that my dinner party will be a success. A smile engulfs my face as I remember mom's old recipe, and I begin to prepare my feast. The savory, sweet smelling aroma flows through the house. Hours later, I hear that anticipated knock on the door, my guest have arrived. "Knock, knock", who is it? I respond.

"It's us, it's us mommy, when can we eat, the cartoons are over, and daddy's sleep."

Box

I'm sitting on my box while my legs are dangling freely beneath me. Oh how wonderful it seems like I could just reach up and touch the sky.
Do I dare stand up I wonder? Yes I'm going for it....
As my knees tremble and my legs shake, I slowly pull myself up onto the box.
I stand up tall, as if I were a tower and look around at everything below me, playfully, I pretend I'm sword fighting and I twirl around and miss my step.
I'm falling off of my box, the birds' scatter, as my feet kick upwards as I slam to the ground in pain, and my box falls on top of me.
Oh my knee, such pain as I find myself now in the box and it's dark, so I struggle to get the box off of me.
97...98...99...100. Here I come, ready or not. The box starts to rise off of me and while I hold my bruised knee, a hand reaches out to help I think.
When I hear tag.....you're out!

Don't

Don't ever say you wonder why you haven't been noticed. You have and been loved by many, especially by Jesus. You are needed and necessary in the lives of many, including mine. I hope this message you'll receive in time, before you give up on life and possibilities, to share with the ones who need your smile, your embrace, your wisdom, your love.

Let my heart beat for you, when yours slow down and it seems to break. Let me comfort you in your darkest hour. I will be discreet and gentle with your emotions. When I reach out please reach back. Let me catch you before you fall, let me pick you up when you hit the bottom. Let me warm you when you feel cold, let me lick your wounds and bandage your pain, let me stop the emotional rain.

Let me show you the sunshine, don't give up, don't give up!!!

The Down Low

When you told me that you were coming over, I was so excited that I felt guilty as if I was going to faint on the spot. It seems like forever that I've adored you from a distance; my heart smiles every time I see your face. I rushed home so fast to prepare for your visit. Hot bubble bath scented candles, soft red light, complimented by beautiful slow music on the radio. I cut up small pieces of watermelon so I could tantalize and feed her supple lips with the sweet, moist, savory fruit. My dream girl finally arrives. I slide slowly off the bed, that later will tell the story of our hot, passionate, sexual encounter, with the intensity of rabbits in heat. As she leaned forward against my bed, I came from behind, while my hands began to grope her pussy and squeeze her body, pulling her closer to me. I press into her velvet skin, trying to merge our flesh into one, as she began to remove the scanty articles of clothing. Fully nude, she climbed into my bed as if a lioness on the prowl and laid there in her nakedness, I felt tightness in my chest. I knew I must not fail to satisfy her, not wanting it to be the last time, caught up in modest shyness that I so cleverly concealed behind the scented chiffon scarf that covered her eyes. I look at her nipples, waiting for my mouth to devour them and her pussy to lavish over, as my fingers slide inwards, my tongue licks her wet, moist, dripping pussy as she sighs "Oooh, Oooh", breathing so slow and so deeply. I allow my tongue to search out and caressingly travel around her body leaving areas to explore later. I feel my own pussy starts to moisten up,

and beads of sweat engulf my breast and cascades down my back. "Oh, I think, this is forbidden fruit, while I don't care, I'm in the moment. How much I crave for her to fuck me, ever so hard, that my pussy screams out into ecstasy as we both are feeling the overwhelming intense desire to have sex. After prolonged foreplay, I return to the dark cavern, where I part her lips and her aroma of body heat drives me to a frenzy. I lick her hot, streaming pussy, while her ass starts to gyrate backwards and forward, as I stretch my hand to reach the
vibrator lying beside me; the low hum , as I turned it on, excites me because I knew it's getting ready to become hot and heavy, as I continue to lap up her pussy juices, as if likened unto a cat with a bowl of milk. I purr as my body screams out to be touched, penetrated, and sucked. I want to fuck like this is my last day on earth. I roll my head sideways and reached up to pinch her nipples; that were standing at attention in anticipation of my touch. We decide to switch places, because I'm already on fire. She spreads my legs wide and went down with her experienced tongue, penetrating my pussy like a penis in frenzy. Oh, I can't contain myself, reaching out to find something to hold onto, as I claw at her arms and hands; she squeezes my hand so firmly. I think this can't be as good as it seems. What the hell kind of lovemaking is this? So passionate, so hot, and so intense. I am loving every minute of it; then I realize, "its lesbian love, am I gay, or should I keep this on the down low."

Can I talk to you?

Hey, do you have a few minutes? I want to share this with you. It's not my plan to flatter you and hope you let your guard down. My emotions are raw and sensitive towards you. I'm flustered and caught up and my body tingles when you are in the room. My breath becomes deep and shallow. When I close my eyes, I still see you. Your body beckons me like a moth to a flame. I know you think I'm intense and overwhelming in my attention. I'm lost in my vulnerability to your essence. I risk putting my feelings out there because I need you to know how deep in my soul that you have stirred up emotions and my feelings are acting on auto pilot. Afraid I've gone too far by sharing too much, it isn't necessary to sex you up; that's just icing on the cake. Moments without you, my heart seems to break. It wasn't my intention to fall this hard. I've taken the right precautions in the past. I've built a wall to protect my heart from the darts of infatuations and needless love encounters that go nowhere. Fear grips my mind as I see the walls crumbling to let you in, to occupy a space that's been empty for too long. Having to face the truth and be honest with myself, I knew I had to love you. The intensity seems like a fantasy within reach; a possible illusion. I don't believe in fairy tales, but I believe there is something special for me and I don't want to miss out on my dream come true. Let me show you how big my heart is, trusting you will be gentle with it; it's been broken before a few times in the past. And though it's on the road to recovery, it can't sustain a crucial hit.

Don't become my nightmare. I don't have it in me to pick up the pieces again. If love isn't there, this thing between us; let it slip away and end, and go back to where our friendship began.

Carousel

Why do I allow myself to continue in this madness, craving for a close relationship while always falling short? I put my heart on my sleeve and you knock it off anytime you want. My soul cries from the inside and your constant apologies are supposed to make me alright. How long can I continue putting up with you?... You say you love me but you treat me like a carousel, going around and round and round. You get on and off at your whim. As my life continues, I reach towards the golden ring, my reward. I reflect how I've been emotionally raped, spiritually abused and drowned in my own salty tears. I hope things will finally change for me because again, I am approaching the golden ring and now it seems in reach. I stretch my arms forward, leaning out while not trying to fall off once again. Oh my, I've got it, I'm so happy. I finally have the band of gold, until I look closely, and see its only brass and tarnished like my life.

Hijacked

Don't try to hijack my feelings. You keep me in bondage and tie me down and then there are times you don't want me around. It's real confusing, just where I stand. All these secrets, is that the plan? You're juggling my emotions at the drop of a hat; I have to wonder should I ever come back. There are others who stole your heart away, causing you drama, it seems, everyday. They have backed you in a corner and you don't know where to turn. Just tell the truth, this lesson you've learned. This relationship was costly as we both know, but in reality, you need to let go. It's causing confusion in your family, and havoc everywhere, this drama, you shouldn't have to bear. I'm your friend, and I'll be here for you, but what road you take, you'll have to choose, unless you want to stay hijacked.

Let me come to your Rescue

When I heard you on the phone, I could hear the tears in your eyes.
You made me so sad when I heard you cry. I asked you what was wrong
and you replied nothing. While I could feel that you felt all alone,
let me come to your rescue.

As I sat on the phone and listened to silence, I heard your whimper and
it cut me to my heart, because you wouldn't let me come to your rescue.

I finally encourage you to talk and tell me what was wrong.
You opened up to me that something was done by someone that you
loved. They hurt you so bad, that it made you sad;
let me come to your rescue.

Don't cry girl, don't cry no more, even though your heart has been torn.
Someone loves you and they are right here, you can let me in and have no
fear. Your heart is precious to me and I'll hold it near.
Why don't you….? Let me come to your rescue!

Toilet Paper

I am sitting on my throne, just waiting to relieve myself. I reach for my toilet paper and I notice that I am low. Reaching down to open my cabinet to retrieve some more toilet paper... I see that I'm down to one roll. This really pisses me off. How could this be? Then I thought, "Oh yeah, I remember now, my neighbors have been borrowing rolls of toilet paper." Immediately, I start thinking...what about the code? You know; the things you are not supposed to borrow. You don't borrow soap. You don't borrow underwear. You don't borrow deodorant, and you don't borrow any damned toilet paper. Haven't you heard about the dollar stores? Or considered taking napkins from Burger King or McDonalds? What about the paper in the shoe box? And if things are really tough...then use newspaper, but, please don't borrow my damned toiled paper. Sometimes I think about just kicking your #$%/?)# ass when you ask me "can I borrow some toilet paper!"

I have to Tell

There's something I have to tell. I want to lick your lips and lick them well.

I want to part them, and go real deep.
Need so much to feel your body heat.

When I'm with you, I'm wound so tight, this brain can't seem to figure it out, and don't care whether it's wrong or right.

I just need some moments with you, I'll even settle if I only had two.

I'm not trying to scare you off, in my brain, all reasoning is lost.

Around my heart, I've built a fence, and my feelings for you are so intense.

I'm on love's highway and you are the boss, do what you will at any cost.

At the intersection of lust and demand,
can't wait to grope you with my greedy little hands.

I'm so glad that it's you that I've found,
I feel like my feet won't touch the ground.

Baby I am enjoying this ride, I must admit,
I don't want it to stop and I don't want it to quit.

Share

As I look over my life and its experiences I think, "What legacy have I left"?

I've always tried to be good and treat others well.
I suffer inside when I see your outward pain.
I love the laughter that feels the air like sunshine upon my face,
but yet I wonder what legacy have I left.

I guess I'll just share this thought and hope it serves you well.
As my eyes grow dim and my memory fades,
this thought comes fresh to my mind.

Never miss out on life and expect nothing but the best, don't settle for less
if you are not happy, regardless.
Don't pretend in your mind that you're in a relationship
if it's only and always one sided.

Love is exciting and fresh and fills your heart with joy and laughter.
And smiles that beam upon your face

So let me share this legacy with you before my memory begins to erase.....

Can you help out a Sistah?

You're always complaining that you want a good man and lover, someone to caress you and love you just right. When I volunteer for the job, you say, "no", but I'm just trying to help out a sistah. You find yourself alone, masturbating, when I'm willing to help out a sistah and you turn me down and say "no." You're always saying that you wish someone would have a nice, hot, bubble bath waiting on you when you get home. I tell you that I'm prepared; I have the soap and want to be your rubber ducky, but you say "no", and I'm just trying to help out a sistah. You're always complaining about money when you know I'm low on cash. I never hear you tell me, "Let me help out a brother." It seems very typical that when there is sex, and no finances, I always hear, "Can you help out a sistah". (But you can't beat a brother for trying.)

I'm not going to Cry

I'm not going to cry. Inside I feel sickened and depressed, tears that burn my eyes, held back at the brink from falling. What just happened here? I'm confused. You're very moody, can't stay in the same room with me. I've done nothing wrong. Just the night before, all was fine, but today, you're different, distant, and aloof. I'm forced to try to figure it out on my own. Do you wish I was someone else? Or is it your own personal guilt that's catching up to you? Yesterday you said you loved me and today you say don't call you anymore. Wow, just crush my feelings; blame me for your issues. You see I'm not going to cry, even thou the tears are at the surface….. Then before I realized it, a tear drop fell.

Dreaming

I breathe inward so slow and so deep while feeling the coolness
with my body heat.
I touch my breast and squeeze them slow,
feeling all the tingling sensations grow.
My heart is beating fast in my chest. But I still caress myself….
While I rest upon my bed, I'll spread my legs open and cradle my head,
now my body continues to yearn and beg...
I'll touch that private space, and my love juices I will not waste.
My nipples get hard as I rise up and down,
twirling my fingers slowly around.
I slide it inwards, so slow and so deep, in that dark cavity,
while my heart beats.
I moan as I think about you loving me all the night through,
lost in my passion because of you.
While passion builds up to a peak, I'm so lost in lust that I can't speak. My
body is on fire and there is smoke,
touching myself again, and then I awoke….

Grandparents

Other people's kids can drive you nuts and have you so stressed out, you think, "Oh fuck! Come and get them and do it quick. I'm so tired and ain't feeling this shit. They don't listen and make a mess, when they do something wrong, they won't confess. Dropping things all on the floor, you shake your head, can't take no more. You find yourself needing a drink, after losing your sedatives down the sink. Your mind is pissed off and you're having a fit; all jumbled from the chaos and shit. The bell finally rings at the door while you think, "Get the hell out, and don't come back no more." You hug and kiss as they exit your place. It's so priceless, the look on your face. But there is always one, who doesn't want to leave. That is the one crying and asking, "Grandma, pleaseeee!"

Some Say

Some poems I write are oh so sweet…
And the message I relay is very deep.
A lot appears to be so x-rated, you either like it or you hate it.
It's hard to read about sex in print, that's why some of you think it stinks.
And because I'm so witty, I get right down to the real nitty-gritty.
Someone said that I was so nasty,
but they had to admit that my stuff was sassy.
And when they read my poems,
they admit, that they get warm just reading my shit.
So I think about the things they've said,
I guess I'm nasty…., but I'm great in bed.

When is it going to End?

You find yourself in a relationship that you need to get out of. Your lover has totally flipped straight out. You've been threatened, financially used up, brought to tears and disrespected, but your silly ass, as soon as you hear their voice, go running, putting everything else on hold. You wish you could kick your own butt, as you think, "Why am I so stupid when it comes to this person." You risk your support system because they are truly tired of this constant drama, but you want your cake and eat it too. Well, I hope you like the weight gain of discontent, the bulge of anxiety, and the enlarged heart of disappointment, and the arms of bruising from being man handled. You pray for peace, but you're bound like a prisoner to your emotions. Finally, you decide to start over and tell your family the truth of the situation and share the dysfunction, so that you can get your power back. With shaky legs, you make your first step, then the next, before you stumble. Instead of getting up, you decide to crawl back into that mess. When is it going to end?

Loved and Lost

Every now and then I wonder what to do.
Then I think about the things concerning me and you.
I wonder why it ended so badly, because inside I am really sad.
Maybe I should have tried harder to tell you just how I felt,
instead of walking away, and keeping things to myself.
I feel lonely without you, and think about you all day long.
I think I've made a mistake, because now it seems you're gone.
I feel miserable inside when I think about your face,
no longer can I kiss you, or hold a sweet embrace.
The days have turned into night and the nights have turned to weeks.
My heart has grown bitter, and my feelings won't let me speak.
It hurts so bad that I loved and lost my friend, afraid to venture out and
seek love once again.

Relationships

I find myself looking into your eyes and they dance and sparkle in the coolness of the night.

My heart races because you're so close to me and the beats pound inside my chest. I try to appear composed, but all the while I'm jumpy and giddy.

Looking at your lips while you talk, as I visualize the softness we would share in that passionate moment of embrace. Your body heat next to mine, while I hold you close to me, and caress your back so gently in my arms.

Rain threatens outside and the clouds grow darker, while I think it's time to go home, yet I don't want to miss a moment with you.

We talk, we giggle; we look at each other,
for what seems like forever before we each turn away.
As I feel the hot, burning, intense heat between us.

Your eyes begin to tear up as I reach out to touch the moisture on your face, and softly wipe your cheek.
Your phone begins to vibrate and you turn to look at me.......

You pause and say....
"But I'm already in a relationship."

Zzzzzz's

Finally some alone time, great so I go get a snack, and prepare to enjoy the quiet while enjoying a wonderful show on the television.
This is great I think, no interruption, phone not ringing; just peaceful; enjoying my show, just how I like it.

Oh here it comes, someone grabbing me on the shoulder, shaking me. I knew it was too good to last.

What! What! I moan, what is it? Oh nothing they reply, just wanted you to wake up.

What do you mean wake up; can't you see I'm watching TV?
No you're not, the TV is watching you.
Zzzzzz's

Rain

I love the rain; it's wonderful, the patter against my window, as the glistering beads of water race down the pane, as in a car race, trying to get to the bottom first. I reach out my hand against the window and peer outwards; many different umbrellas in all shades, going to and fro, concealing the faces beneath them. Kids running to find shelter as their clothes cling to their bodies. Across the street, people hide under the store awning from protection from the rain, while waiting for the bus to appear. Car horns honking, the excitement is in the air. At the newspaper stand, the paper and magazines are getting drenched while the clerk hustles to cover them with plastic. As I pull my coat tighter, a soft chuckle escapes my lips. The car pulled up to the light and splashed water all over the man standing at the curb. As he began to swear and frantically try to wipe the water from his clothes, he looks over in my direction and I crouch in my seat so he'll not see the amusement upon my face. Moments pass when I hear thump upon my door. Knock, knock, I turn around to be sure it's my door where the knocking sounds come from, and then there's silence.

I hear the knocking sounds again against my door, cautiously I open my door and my son stands there, with his umbrella in his hand and reaches out to me and said, "Dad come on, let's get out of the rain, you have already splashed me and I'm drenched."

What do you want?

You want me to understand you. How can I do what you never could? It starts with you, and being honest with yourself. "Do you want your cake so that you can eat it too? An emotional roller coaster is what I find myself on…, yet I never purchased a ticket. I just looked at you and my world changed. Some things are brand new, while others are still the same. Penalized for the damage in your life, I reach out to you, as you pull back. How do I understand you? You close up into your shell, retreating from the emotional battles of life and love… "What do you want…, or is the problem you just don't know?"

Tracy

Tracy works at the post office, a beautiful teller. She deals with your problems in all kinds of weather. Giving out stamps and weighing boxes, talking to knuckleheads, and some were hostile. She keeps a smile on her face, and it's beautiful to see, she's special to many, and that includes me. You may can't tell I think she's wonderful, but I can't say it, because I'm too humble.

Standing on her feet, all day long.... Bending over boxes, till her back is worn. Fighting through pain while doing her job, but inside shed her silent sobs. She takes pride in her dress and looking so well, uniform crispy from what I can tell. She works hard to support her kids, with a missing dad, while she's mother...instead. Doing all she can to pick up the slack, but that isn't fair and I think its whack. She continues daily bringing happiness and joy, while she stands on the miserable floor. Now I'm so honored and glad that she's my friend. I look for her face each time I go in. The days that she's off, I know she is missed, I hope she's relaxing and that is my wish.

What If?

What if you came home and I was lying on my back…
What would you say, damn girl, you look fat.
What if you came home and I had gained a little weight,
would you be honest or would you be fake?
What if I farted and the smell burnt your eyes?
Would you start running or visibly cry?
What if I was broke and lost all my funds?
Would the party be over and you think I was dumb?
What if I asked you…baby could you wear my dress?
Would you think it was cool and yell "hell yes"?
What if I told you I couldn't drive anymore,
would you think it's a trick or think it's a ploy?
What if I told you to buy me some hair,
would you just do it, or would you be scared?
What would you do if we had a big fight?
Would you make up with me or stay out all night?
What if I broke the favorite record you had?
Would you be sad, or would you be mad?
What if I was jealous and acted a fool?
What would you do, or would you be cool?
What if I said that I was born a man?
What would you do, would you cancel our plans?
What would you do if I suddenly became rich?
Would you jump up and down and yell, "Oh shit".
What would you do if I ended this poem?
Would you say don't do it, just keep it going on?
But the time has come and I've reached my end,
As now I bid farewell to you my friends.

Bitch

The salty taste of my tears once again, the headache simmering, right below the surface. My soul feels depressed and I don't want to go out. What is it about me I wonder that has me caught up again? I wonder what has me caught up into another dead end relationship. Don't I do enough? I think I'm attentive, clean, trustworthy, and devoted to your every whim. I'm here when you need to be listened to; I support your ideas. I lose sleep over and for you and it seems that all I get from you are morsels of Kibbles and Bits, the food you give to your dog. No matter how often you mistreat your dog, they are happy to see you and run towards you. Even though I find myself doing the same thing, I need you to know...that...I'm not your bitch!

Saturday Morning

As I open my eyes, I breathe in so slowly and deeply. I turn over and my hands rub my eyes so that I may focus. My bed feels so wonderful as I lay here in my nakedness with the coolness of the sheet against my skin. Instinctively, I rub my breast in a circular motion, while taking my hand up and down towards my throat. My eyes flutter as I remember the night before; I remember how good it felt to masturbate, how I touched every crevice with my toys, the heavy breathing while I plunged deeply inside of me with my dildo, pulling it in and out so slowly, as my pussy shot off rockets of ecstasy, my fingertips, pinching my nipples, because I love pain on my nipples as I soar in my passion. My pussy was so wet I could hear the sucking motion of my juices when I tried to pull out. I turn myself over and climb on top of my pillow so that my pussy rubs abrasively against it, while I slowly and deliberately fuck myself with my imitation dick thrust so deep within the walls of my vagina. I feel the urge to scream out in pleasure as I approach that point of release. Oh how good it feels as I bite my lips and pinch harder on my nipples and I thrust harder into my pillow as my pussy violently pulsates and trembles as my strength leaves my body and I drift off to dream land. My chest rises and falls until I realize its' day, as I open my eyes and stretch out my arms, and think what a beautiful day; it's Saturday morning.

What would you do?

What would you do if I said I wanted you?
Would you give me your heart, or would I be blue?
What would you do if I said just give me a chance, cause
when I look at you, my heart seems to dance.
What would you do, if I called you tonight,
would you let me fulfill your fantasy, and let me hold you so tight?
What would you do if I left you alone?
Would you break down, and tell me to come home?
What would you do if you realized our love was all that?
Would we together run and never look back?
Not dwelling on the stuff that happened in the past,
living for today, furious and fast.

Upset

It upset you because you thought I was mad.
It upset you and made you sad.
Haven't you learned from the past, this thing between us is going to last.
Our relationship may evolve in a lot of ways, but as long as you need me,
I will stay.
Don't you know I want the best for you?
That's why you don't need to choose.
Loving you is the easiest thing I've ever done.
It takes more than some crap to make me run.
And as we get older, and that we will do,
just remember my love was really true.

Milestones

The first kiss, the first sexual encounter, your first love, are memories
that are filled with excitement, fear and uncertainty.
Years have rolled by and your memories are fresh as dew,
as if they were just moments before.

Being naïve and nervous, venturing into your growth at a speed faster
than light.

First job, first car, first marriage, first child; struggling day in and day out to
finally avoid that foreclosure notice on your home.

Heartaches, death, illnesses, regrets, baptism, relocation,
children going off to war,

Stock market crash, earthquakes, vehicle accidents, retirement funds,
401K, bankruptcy.

Mail fraud, credit card solicitations, telemarketers, thunderstorms,
blizzards, weddings.

Blowing out candles on a birthday cake, making a wish…, I wish,
I wish for a few more milestones.

Have You?

Have you ever loved someone that never loved you back?
As much as it hurts you continue in your madness; longing for a touch,
a glance, a smile, just to realize the look is for someone behind you.
You turn around and your heart drops
because inside you've been let down and ashamed.
You hope no one sees the flutter of your eyelids
that holds back the simmering tears.
You hold your head back. Inside you quiver, trying to leave as gracefully as
possible; all eyes seem to penetrate you.
All laughter seems to be about you. But is it you?
So is it your imagination. You cling to what used to be, afraid,
but you need to walk into your destiny.
Have you ever wondered, have you?
Ever been in the place in life where the beginning was the end?

Before you Eat

This story is about my friend who had the choice between two different men. I told her to look at the menu before she decides what to eat. Some like meats, but I like sweets.

Give me eye candy, not trick or treat.

Now I'll call one of them butter because he's real smooth, this man has his stuff together, plus he ain't a fool. He has a nice home, with finances too, dresses real sharp and he would look good next to you.

Now, this other one is very plain, kind of fat with no personal gain. His credit is shot and his place is not neat. All you get from him are words that sound sweet.

Call me crazy if you will, but my choice is easy, and I would chill… with butter if I had a choice. I need a prince and not a frog; I'm not a pet owner, so I don't need a dog. So if I was going to think about what I would eat, whether my choice was meat, or sweets. I would prefer eye candy as my personal treat, if I had to choose before I could eat.

The First Cup

Oh how I think about that first cup in the morn, as I sip on my brew, it goes down so warm, as I ponder about the things that I would like to do. I'm sitting and sipping on my warm cup of brew.
And then when I want a really special treat, I get out the Danish, because they are so sweet. Sometimes it's a bagel and sometimes its toast, my drink of choice, well..., I love tea the most? What a wonderful way that I will start my day, with that warm sensation and a smile on my face.

Searching

What are you searching for? And what's the pursuit of happiness?
Are you searching for love, and where do you look?
Are you searching for stability, and how do you make it happen?
Are you searching for your lover, and why do you deserve to be loved?
Are you searching for the truth, but you refuse to see it?
Are you searching for a connection, because you feel unplugged?
Are you searching for family, because you feel all alone?
Are you searching for money, and the pleasures that it brings?
Are you searching for peace, because you do things too extreme?
Are you searching to find, what satisfies your craving inside?
Are you searching for yourself, because that's the person you hide?

When?

When is it my turn to be that special one?
When is it my turn to whom you would run?
When is it my turn to feel all aglow?
Am I expressing my feelings a little to slow?
When is it my turn that you ask me to stay?
When is it my turn beside you I will lay?
When is it my turn that you dry my tears?
When life's ups and downs creates some fears.
When is it my turn for you to become my mate?
When is it my turn that you know it is fate?
When is it my turn for a love that is brand new?
My heart races, just looking at you.
When is it my turn to have that final break?
Wanting a good relationship, I can't wait.
When is it my turn that all things align?
Things' going perfect and all is just fine?
When is it my turn to just sit and grin?
If its not now, can you tell me when?????

Loneliness

Loneliness is depressing and everyone goes through it. It consumes your mind in a state of depression. You feel unloved and uncared for. You resent the fact that you're missing out on attention as well, even though your story, you wouldn't even tell. Maybe you think it's something wrong with you and you want to change some of the things that you do, so you'll be appreciated and noticed.

You rethink over and over and find fault in yourself, comparing yourself to others and looking for flaws because you are lonely and no one calls. The phone that once rang hardly rings anymore and there is no one knocking on the door. Occasionally, a relative calls, but it really doesn't help because all you have to tell is nothing at all. You have no plans and you wonder why no one thinks you are special.

Finally, you get that call from one of your friends. They ask you to go out, so you think, "I might as well," because you have no plans. You hang out a while because this is the best offer you've had all day, stopping by a few stores; sightseeing.

Well, a couple of hours have passed and your friend tells you they have to go home because they have special plans for the evening and your depression begins to come back. While you're driving back towards home, your friend asks you to detour past their house, they want to share something with you. So you think, "why not." I need to see something special, after all, it's my birthday and no one remembered or noticed.

While you wait for your friend to open the door,

you look around and think, what a miserable day.
Everyone I thought cared about me forgot my birthday.
Fine, ok, let's go in, and, to my surprise I hear, "Happy Birthday."

Just putting it out there

I want you and it ain't about sex, but when I'm near you,
it makes me sweat.

You make me lose my mind. I'm not tripping and I'm not lying.
My mind is all mixed up with crap, don't know if I'll recover,
or ever come back.

I used to be on top of my game; kept my emotions in check.
But not any longer cause I haven't got you yet.

When you smile at me, it pulls a trigger; my love for you,
it grows bigger and bigger.

Thinking about you at night, it.....
seems you're running all through my dreams.
If I don't watch myself and try to hold back,
I'll mess around and have a love attack.

It seems you put me on a shelf..., yeah, got the message,
you love someone else.
When things don't work out for you like they sometimes do,
then dust me off...I'll still be here too.

Circles

You got me going in circles, and half the time I don't know what to do. My life seems to be consumed always with you.

I know you love another and that burns to the heart, so I suffer in silence, afraid to depart.

I stand there waiting with my heart in my hand, trying to figure out my next crazy plan.

How to woo you and keep your interest peaked, while a glimpse of your body, I'll often seek.

I salivate at the thought of touching your chest, and feeling your skin next to my breast.

Got me going in circles, ain't that a trip?

When can I get some more?

Men, have you ever wanted to be fucked so good that you would hope it last forever? Well I've thought about it as well. Imagine if you will, we are together on a comfortable furry rug, on the floor, soft lights in the background, with romantic love songs playing tunes in the air. We are both freshly bathed and smelling great, lying together in our nudity with a bowl of strawberry and whipped cream within reach. Your hands are touching every part of my body playfully as I reach out toward your manhood and pull up and down on your penis, while firmly gripping your dick within my hands. I roll over towards you as my round, soft ass juts out and feel your hands surround them while your fingers slide in between them to find my hot, wet, slimy pussy that you thrust your fingers so deeply into....As good as it feels, I reposition myself so that my ass is facing your waiting tongue while my mouth finds your throbbing wet dick to swallow. With my hot tongue, I inch your penis slowly into my mouth while sucking so slow and firmly as my hands are sliding up and down and up and down, your dick begins to get larger and larger. I have to yawn to take all of your manhood into my mouth. Oh how good it feels, you're eating my pussy and I'm sucking your dick. As we both begin to tremble, we decide it's time for you to put your dick inside of me deep. You reach out for the vibrator and I turn over and rise up on my knees in doggy style. I can't wait. My breasts are heaving up and down in anticipation. You spread my ass cheeks wide and slowly you slide your dick into my waiting hole, while you put the vibrator within my tingling, tight, waiting pussy. Oh how good this shit feels; both holes are being fucked. I'm licking my lips in hunger for more. Give it to me, fuck me hard. I pinch my own nipples and I hear you moan with excitement. As you are fucking me so hard and so good, pushing your dick inside my ass deeper and deeper, I can't contain myself.

My body is literally on fire, sweat is dripping and the bed sheets are slipping, while you're riding the hell out of me. I yell, "Get it baby, get it baby; fuck the shit out of me! Make that pussy hurt." "Oh, Oh, Oh", escapes your lips as you rub my breasts and squeeze them so tight while you are fucking me in my ass. I say, "Go faster, go faster." You're pushing your dick inside of me; we look like two dogs stuck together needing to be doused with hot water. I'm experiencing some great, animalistic, fire hot, off the wall, fucking that I haven't had in a long time; I'm being sexed up so good and I can't hold back. Oh shit, I'm coming. I shake, I tremble, I can't breathe; my body tingles all over as my heart pounds in my chest. I'm sweating as my pussy throbs and tingles; I'm in heaven and loving every minute. While my strength is being sucked out of me to the point I can no longer move or speak, but lay there drained, and reflect on how good it was and think, "when can I get some more."

Sleepy

I'm so sleepy; don't know what to do, can't keep my eyes open,
thou I'm thinking about you.
Stayed up too long, trying to finish my book,
I didn't eat and I didn't even cook.
I was at my buddy's house, just spending some time,
Kicking it with her, while writing more rhymes.
Her kids watching television, and sprawled out on the couch
She yelled at her son and I immediately thought, "ouch".
Made me remember when my mom called me out, in front of folks,
and that made me pout.
Well, I'm older now and that's in the past and these kids will have to
understand, today.... their problems, they won't last.

My Poems

I was told that I had some talent.
For writing poems there seemed no challenge.

They pop in my head, soon right out of bed.
Trying to hold back, the words roll out instead.

The thing I'll say about my poems is this.
They start one way and end with a twist.

Blending my thoughts that are in my head,
I'll do till the day that they find me dead.

They are written for pleasure, no matter whether you like them or not.

But I've been told that my poems are really, really hot.

Keep waiting on an Apology

If you are waiting on an apology, because the truth sounds so abrasive…then keep waiting. I'm not going to justify the truth with a lie. You need a reality check, wake up call if you think for one minute, that I will allow you to censure the truth. Come on now! you know… that person will go there. The realization is that it's an ugly thought in your brain, and even more so when verbalized. I will not apologize for the truth. The truth stands on it's on. You are supposed to be special to that person; yet time and time again, you're hurt and threatened. Yes they are capable of hurting you again. How many lies does it take, before you get the message? Stop letting them drag you down into that pit of despair, and frantic behavior. I've been there for you, don't you remember? I'm not going to apologize for me telling you to leave that nut along…it's not going to happen. I was there when they put those tears in your eyes. I was there when you wanted to give up on life, because your burdens seemed too great to bear. I was there in the wee hours of the morning, trying to comfort you. When it seemed all hoped was lost. And I'm here to get you through this rough patch, when you want to see the good in everyone. No! I'm not going to apologize for that…. you'll have to keep waiting.

Fat not Phat!

Let me tell you about being fat and chunky with a pretty face. The only problem I had was a cellulite disgrace. Wondering when things turned south and my body went to hell, eating all that junk, only I could tell. Working out only brings me sweat and tears. Now being fat is my very worst fear.. People judging me when I eat a candy bar, my legs are fat, and can't walk very far. But I like sweets, just like you do, feet all swollen and ran over in my shoes. Toes screaming at me "damn you! damn you!" Hate looking at a bathroom scale, peep over my shoulder and see nothing but tail. My stomach has dropped to my waist, fat like a turkey that needs to be braised. When you go to visit it isn't much fun, to see people hide their food while they run. When you sit in a chair, you're really not sure, if your fat ass will hit the floor. You huff and puff when you try to get up, people stare at you and whisper "oh fuck!" and kids as honest as they are, will point at you and laugh real hard. So I guess the thing I really want to do, is continuing eating my candy bar.....point my finger..... and say "SCREW YOU!"

When you're Down and Out

"You want me to be on hold, but I had to stop seeing you, cold turkey if you will". Yet as much as I thought I needed you and desired you, it became apparent I needed God in me. My focus was in worldly admirations instead of spiritual revelations. We all have been through this from time to time, caught up in the glamour, the pretty face, smooth talkers, sexual explosions, and untapped resources…then there are times you just want to be needed. Aloneness will have you twisted, spending your money trying to buy love…when it can't be bought. Love is given freely, yet as wonderful as it makes you feel, so often it's taken for granted. In my hour of desperation, while looking and hoping for someone to cling to, I thought, "why not give God a chance." I've made too many mistakes on my own, and at this point there's nothing else to lose. I've been talked about, cheated on, embarrassed, and ashamed, and at the point of giving up and letting go. Even though I feel disrespected, beaten down, and broken, I offer this empty shell, cracked and worn; laced with the stains of my tears. And… at the point of total despair, while Satan whispers in my ear, "nobody wants you but me", a thunderous voice, proclaims, "Stop! Satan get thee behind me, All ye who are burden and heavy laden, come unto me, and I will give you rest."

Accountable

In the heat of the night as I lay in my nakedness, my mind thinks about you, and where we are as a couple. Then I reflect on previous conversations held; remember, you were the one who didn't want to define our relationship, "let's just be friends". Through my pain and disappointment I try to let go. I allow myself the amusement of feeding my starving ego at the whim of another who wants to be in that important spot held by you, yet unappreciated. My love didn't fit the timetable of your chaos, but secretly you yearn for the tenderness I offered and secretly wished it was from the one who damaged your love. Confused, while yet needing to be held, caressed, and protected from the emotional sadness that has gripped your soul in bondage, you turn to me. No longer am I willing to watch you cry in agony, desperate for a solution, where there seems to be none. I find myself tormented in my own struggles to be there for you…knowing my place is on the back burner of your heart. Just once I would like to be considered first. I've been told that when people interact, it's considered a type of relationship. Why has Webster, Random House or any dictionary for that matter led me to believe that I was in a relationship? Why didn't I look up the word foolish instead? That's how I feel. I decide to dry my own tears, and speak wisdom into my… lonely soul. Learn to love yourself first, so you will appreciate the love of another. It's time to venture out, no longer a prisoner to your thoughts, and settling for second place. Realize that if together isn't so good then being alone can't be too bad. It's time to be accountable.

It's Time

It's time I change some things about me.

Sitting in my chair, I take a good hard look at myself. I'm stripped from the facade of the always me complex. Completely exposed and humbled by my fragile emotions and realities, I search to find what makes me tick and what I should expect of others. As I lean back, close my eyes and take a deep breath, I am surprised at the realization that what one needs… they seldom want. The things you want, isn't always needed…."Yes I do need to change, it's time."

Relationships are like Candy

Ever wanted someone, but you were a little intimidated. Because of the sour exterior, liken unto a jawbreaker piece of candy. The outside' doesn't always taste as sweet as you go thru the layers. However the inside is chewable and doable. We all have layers to our personality, some quite bitter and tart to the taste. There are times you wonder do you want to continue or spit out the unpleasantness. Have you ever wondered why some relationships last for decades, and some only a few years. Others last a few months, and some after a few thrills. Maybe you're like a jawbreaker piece of candy. The outside taste bad, while the inside is like I said, "so sweet" or maybe... you're just.... rude and crude!

Hospital Visits

Visits to the hospital aren't what they use to be. I've seen some crazy things going on; things I just could not believe. People come to the hospital, and literally eat the food off of your tray. "Can I have your Jell-O; are you going to drink your juice?" Some real greedy butts, begging and looking at you, at that point you wish that they would just go away. Why do I need to have a headache on this very day? While giving no concern to where they sit, visitors plop on the edge of your bed, weighing you down, while ignoring your pain levels. Some come to visit with nothing in their hands, and don't, ask you if you need anything. Stingy as you can see....think about it. They steal your lotions and your soap; even the latex gloves that the staff uses, all while having the gall to take the patient's personal belongings. What knuckleheads, what a joke. Then there are the ones that sit in the corner, and look all glum...I'd rather that they go instead of looking so dumb. Where are the balloons, cards and the gifts; some of the things you expect to find on your hospital wish list? Lying in a hospital bed really ain't fun, being stuck with needles while your veins start to run. Now the worst thing about this experience, which is true, is receiving that awful bill addressed to you. Now while you're in the hospital, and down in the dumps, you are lying on your rump and your spirit has sunk. Think about the bright side of this, all the nuisance calls that you will miss. Bed not made up, and no dishes to clean. Being pampered and spoiled and feeling serene.

TERRY LYLE

Things you Think About Through my Eyes

Have you ever looked in my eyes and wondered what was behind them? Have you ever walked in my shoes and couldn't stand the pain? Do you know what crosses I have to bear? Have you ever looked outside of your situation, to try and feel someone else's pain? Or do you just be tripping to be tripping? These are the questions that I've thought about. On many occasions, sometimes I wonder why I continue to deal with you; sometimes I wonder if you're ever going to change. Sometimes I wonder is it me? What is it about me that looks for something difficult to fix? What is it about me that can't settle for the easy choices in life? Why do I always find myself in the middle of stuff? Is my celestial role to be a fixer of broken and wounded souls? Why can't I just cruise down easy street? Some of these things I have to think, and ponder why this is; what's really going on? What's the purpose, and what's the plan? Where am I heading, is this a dead end street? Can I turn around, and run in the opposite direction? Is it too late? Or are these twists in the road on life's highways? Or is this another pothole. I'm eagerly willing to fix?

Sneaking Around

Have you ever been guilty of sneaking around? I have and here's my story.

I found myself one day just thinking about, when was the last time I had that hot, climbing the wall type of lovemaking. It seemed like an eternity, and masturbating was getting old quick. So first thing I did was to freshen myself up, dress nicely and go on the prowl. I felt really positive; I had received a few stares and comments of approval. But I had already spied my prey. Now sneaking around involves two aspects. Your desire to go on the hunt, and the prey wanting to be captured, makes for many tantalizing maneuvers. Allthough they are secret desires by most, to be sought after in a romantic way; you'll find it cloaked in secrecy. Initially the most powerful thing is the first glance, and how long that they continue to look before turning away. Subtle changes in their body language are a good sign. Their speech pattern is it confused, fast, nervous or never ending. These are actually positive signs, it shows that you've been noticed and have made an impact. You're ready to open that door a little farther. Now back to my story; time, including plenty of observation, before taking that risk, was what I did to capture him. First I was an attentive listener, waiting for the little bits of information to seep out, on their dos and don'ts, likes and dislikes. I became sympathetic to their issues. It's always imperative to look refreshed and inviting in a subtle way, while being very coy in your attempts. Never want to spook your prize off. With a deep breath, I'm ready to take that next step, time for the smile and comforting words. Seeing how my approach up to this point has been effective, now I'll send my first gift. Starting off small is always good, because it doesn't come off scary, and they like you for the gesture. Never hang around to long; it gives them more time to think about your positive demeanor. Continue in your efforts to be enchanting, until week two of your first gift. Now it will be clear whether your prey will let their guard down or not, at this point.

The ball is now in your court, you plan a special evening, which will end in romance with ambience. Knowing that your partner will feel some remorse about cheating, or the unexpected but visualized desired turn of events, you still continue. The evening is magical, everything went smoothly. Better than I could ever hope for, extremely erotica. Oh the desire in me has become so overwhelming, I could hardly breathe. Yet not wanting to let this end, I know that I must. As I get up to sneak off, into the night, I find my hands bound, as well as my feet. Confusion takes over and I wonder what is this? My wallets empty, my clothes are gone, and my keys are missing. I've just been jacked, hunted down like a prey, while I thought I was the one sneaking around…It was me who was pimped.

Perception

Perception, that curious viewpoint into the mind...I guess it's what you call your own personal reality. What's your reality? Hypothetically let me share two separate takes on the same scenario. First visualize I'm in a room and the temperature is 78 degrees, I'm hot and clammy, my skin is sweaty. Slow shallow, and labored is my breathing, as my nipples cling to my clothing. I begin to wipe the sweat off of me. Miserable day you may think. Now here is scenario number two; my moist skin glistens as I slowly trace the outline of the sweat on my neck. My fingers gently travels down between the crevice of my breast, as my hands lay there unable to move, while I breathe slow and deeply. My nipples cutely poke thru the silk of my blouse. A covering of heat intensified the sultry 78 degree room temperature. How sensuous is that picture? Let me venture off into another detour into perceptions. I've told my significant other that I love them; I would like them to inform me of changes in their movement throughout the day, for safety reasons. I'm overwhelmed with unbridled excitement of our next encounter, while I secretly wish to be able, to bring them sunshine at every moment. How I wish I could pluck a star out of the sky and give it to them, as well as be available to them at a moments notice. This is perception number two; valid as well. My significant other is in love with me. Fact two every time I'm not in their presence, I have to give an itinerary of my movements. Only time they appear happy is when they see everything that I do. They always make their selves available to me when I beckon, but that's fine. If they love me, then they should. I only want to know where they are if I need something. It's good to know they are always near. I don't believe that I'm being selfish, I'm grown why should I have to be accountable? If a person's in love then what action or road seems more appropriate? "The answer really lies in… your perceptions".

www.ingramcontent.com/pod-product-compliance
Ingram Content Group UK Ltd.
Pitfield, Milton Keynes, MK11 3LW, UK
UKHW020139250726
13967UKWH00002B/746

9 781425 184551